The Past Won't Stay Behind You

The Past Won't Stay Behind You

POEMS BY
SAMUEL HAZO

The University of Arkansas Press
Fayetteville   1993

Copyright 1993 by Samuel Hazo

All rights reserved
Manufactured in the United States of America

97   96   95   94   93   5   4   3   2   1

This book was designed by Gail Carter using the typeface Caslon.

The paper used in this publication meets the minimum requirements of the American National Standard for Permanence of Paper for Printed Library Materials Z39.48-1984. ♾

Library of Congress Cataloging-in-Publication Data

Hazo, Samuel John.
   The past won't stay behind you / by Samuel Hazo.
     p.   cm.
   ISBN 1-55728-279-X (alk. paper). — ISBN 1-55728-280-3 (alk. paper)
   I. Title.
PS3515.A9877P36   1993
811'.54—dc20   92-31379
                                                                       CIP

To Paul Mellon

Grateful acknowledgment is made to *The American Scholar, Tar River Poetry, Talisman, The Critic, The Southern Review, The Pittsburgh Post-Gazette, Four Quarters,* and *Painted Bird* in which some of these poems first appeared. "War News Viewed in the Tropics" was initially broadcast on National Public Radio's "Morning Edition."

Contents

Amazement This Way Lies 3

The Real Reason for Going
    Is Not Just to Get There 5

Whatever Happened to Defiance? 8

On the Eve of the First Shot 10

War News Viewed in the Tropics 11

The Courage Not to Talk 13

Seaward 15

And Nowhere Shall We Go 17

The Vow We Breathe 19

Lovemakers 21

One Flesh 23

Partings 25

How Married People Argue 27

Two Against the Mountain 30

Embracing Willa 32

En Route 33

All Mirrors Show the World Reversed 35

The Night Before the Snow 37

Pipedream 39

The Best Place in America to Be on Saturdays   *41*

The Year of the Horse   *44*

Vietnam   *47*

Whatever Makes It Happen Makes It Last   *49*

Not Even Solomon . . .   *51*

The Wait When the Patient Is You   *53*

If I Were a Chef, I'd Say   *55*

The University of All Smiles   *58*

Stingers   *60*

Six-Sevenths   *62*

Putting Away the Lost Summer   *64*

Your Death Is in the Making
  As You Make Your Life   *66*

The Most You Least Expect   *68*

At Midnight There Are No Horizons   *70*

The Past Won't Stay Behind You

Amazement This Way Lies

    You're less assured by what
       assured you totally at twenty.
    Questions outnumber answers now.
    Some questions you can answer.
    Others you live with, and that's
       your answer.
                 You search for Whitehead's
    "values in a world of chance"
    only to discover that "perfection
    is beyond us, that life's a comedy
    for those who think, a tragedy
    for those who feel."
                     Like everyone
    you're left to deal with "the least
    important, but the most demanding . . ."
Six miles overhead, a man
    is forking salad from a molded
    tray.
        A thousand miles east,
a trough in the Atlantic plunges
seven miles deep.
               Berlin's
asleep, Beirut's awake,
Bombay's at lunch, and Brisbane's
almost finished with a day you've
yet to start.
           You think of all
those people, all that water,
all that space . . .

            And then
you think how small is this
summation to the sun.
                 And then
how small the sun to all
the suns of Jupiter.
                    You reach
that point where even the imagination
buckles.
          You're left alone
with wonder—the speechlessness of wonder . . .
Many must share this malady.

The Real Reason for Going Is Not Just to Get There

    Killarney's maps are for the unredeemed.
      The hidden land awaits the stumblers
        and the temporarily confused who find
        their destinations as they go.
    In Dingle there's a history
      bone-final as the faith
      that founded Gallarus.
                        All
    that survives is what was there
      when Gallarus began: God,
      man, sheep, and stone
      and stone and stone.
                    Dingles
    ago, the starvers saw their lips
      turn green from chewing grass
      before they famished in their beds.
    Their hovels bleach like tombs
      unroofed and riven by the sea.
    If only all the stones were beige
      or marble-white . . .
                    The fading
    grays seem unforgiving as a fate
      that only wit or tears
      or emigration can defeat.
    Sheep graze over graves.
    Loud gulls convene on garbage
      dumps.
                In Galway, Cashel
    and Tralee, I fish the air

for what it is that makes
the Irish Irish.
                    Is it Seamus
speaking Sweeney's prayer
in Howth and telling me of Hopkins,
"the convert," buried in Glasnevin?
Is it how it sounds to sing
the music in a name: Skibbereen,
Balbriggan, Kilbeggan, Bunratty,
Listowel, Duncannon, Fermanagh,
and Ballyconneely?
                    Is it Joyce's
map of metaphors that makes
all Dublin mythical as Greece?
Is it cairns of uniambic and unrhyming
rocks transformed by hand
into the perfect poem of a wall?
Is it the priest near death
who whispered, "Give my love
to Roscommon, and the horses
of Roscommon"?
                    It is because
the Irish pray alike for "Pope
John Paul, our bishop Eamon,
and Ned O'Toole, late of Moycullen"?
Inside God's house or out
their sadder smiles say the world,
if given time, will break your heart.
With such a creed they should

believe in nothing but the wisdom
of suspicion.
                Instead they say,
"Please God," and fare ahead
regardless of the odds to show
that life and God deserve at least
some trust, some fearlessness, some courtesy.

Whatever Happened to Defiance?

    People you will never want to know
        are telling you to vote, enlist,
        invest, travel to Acapulco,
        buy now and pay later, smoke,
        stop smoking, curb your dog,
        remember the whale, and praise
        the Lord.
                Like windshield wipers
        they repeat themselves.
                       Because
        they tell but never ask, you learn
        to live around them just to live.
    You understand why Paul Gauguin
        preferred Tahiti to the bourgeoisie
        of France.
                But then Tahiti's
        not the answer any more,
        and frankly never was.
                   This leaves
        you weighing Schulberg's waterfront
        philosophy: "You do it to him
        before he does it to you."
    Reactionary, you admit, but nature's
        way, the way of the world
        where he who wins is always
        he who loses least and last . . .
    But if you're bored by triumph
        through attrition, imitate you may
        the strategy of Puck.

                Listen
carefully to all solicitations, smile
and respond in classical Greek.
It's devious, but then it gives
    you time to smell the always
    breathing flowers.
                Or to watch
dissolve into the mystery of coffee
the faceless dice of sugar
cubes.
    Or to say how damn
remarkable it is that every
evening somewhere in this world
a play of Shakespeare's being staged
with nothing to be won but excellence.

On the Eve of the First Shot

    I've never seen so many generals,
    and none in uniform.
              This general
  talks nuclear.
                This general predicts.
This general's for royalty and oil-ty.
This general's too fat.
                He breathes
  like something leaking air.
This general says do it now
  or do it later, but, for God's
  sake, do it . . .
                Mothers are silent.
Fathers are silent.
            Young
  wives who kiss their husbands
  on the docks are silent.
                Elsewhere
  in studios, on radio, in stereo,
  the generals are noisy with solutions.
No one can silence them.
After the war, they'll
  tell us all the same
  predictions in reverse, proving
  the war developed as they said,
  with due allowance for the deals,
  the drudgery, the dollars and the dead.

War News Viewed in the Tropics

    It seems like melodrama beamed
      from Mars: two Presidents like goats
      about to butt, marines in bunkers
      reading every letter's every word,
      tank captains squinting
      from their turrets "somewhere in Arabia."
Among mimosa, bougainvillea
      and coconuts, what sucks me back
      into this nausea for news?
                            Remembering
    Seferis, I can say my country
    wounds me anywhere I go.
What's happening to us?
Is this how America's century
    ends?
        Why are we now
    so quick to kill however slowly
    and so slowly quick to sweat
    for peace?
            For months we've acted
    like the new crusaders, righteous
    as Barbarossa and the British kings.
The true cross of our cause
    is true for everyone
    because we say it is.
Not that we're trapped between
    a tyrant and a sheikh with eighty
    sons.
          Not that we've bought

    accomplices we call allies.
                    Not that
the sand will claim our camps
as surely as the years made wrecks
of Richard's castles near the coast.
Not that we've made a hoax
    of history . . .
                  Meanwhile, old Moscow's
come apart like Rome, Constantinople
and Madrid.
             Eleven-time-zones
wide, all Russia begs
like Ethiopia for bread.
                  The second
world's careening into bits.
Here in the third, the islanders
respond to our new order
with their own.
              They've started
hoarding kerosene.
             They pray
unhopefully for peace.
              They say
the worst is always unforeseen.

The Courage Not to Talk

    Students may thank you for a word
      they say you said at the right
    moment.
                Nod and pretend
    you remember.
                       Nothing is lost
    by failing to be totally exact . . .
A kiss from your son may stop
    you in mid-thought to prove
    that life is love or it's a waste.
Be grateful.
            Not everyone arrives
    at such assurances . . .
                      Victims
    in Palestine may suffer on
    for being who they are.
                    Recall
    the last beatitude whose prophecy
    is justice.
              Something will change,
    and if you're not alive
    to see it, what's the loss?
Since gratitude and love and pain
    are languages you learn to speak
    by keeping still, keep still.
Silence has a million dialects,
    and every dialect's a mystery,
    and every mystery's a reason
    to be glad you're listening.

                              Practice
for mystery each night before
you sleep.
       Think past your eyelids,
past the ceiling, past the roof
and clouds and into spaces
so immense that no geometry
but God's can measure them.
Or else imagine you're about
to die.
       The words you want
to say are hiding on the other
side of death.
               They tell you
they're too sacred to be heard.
They say the only word
you need to speak is breath.

Seaward

    We watch the sheer steadiness
       of what the thunder prophesied.
The leaves turn greener
    as they drip.
            Roof shingles
    glisten like the scales of trout
    an inch below the surface.
A neighbor's dog keeps sniffing
    for some other somewhere
    that is dry, drier, driest,
    chews at his chain, then settles
    for a slow soaking.
              Watching
    the dog, we see ourselves.
The rain turns allegorical.
The chained identity of who
    we are is all that stays us
    through the worst of storms.
We search for some reprieve.
We fail.
       We make the best
    of things . . .
            Later, we may talk
    of rain as just another element.
But now it makes us think
    the earth's the past, the sky's
    the future, while the rain and all
    its fatherings from sea to sewer
    are the present . . .

                Is it
because we're nine-tenths water
that we feel this way?
                     Oceans
and rivers draw us to themselves
like love.
           Swimming, we're
as much at sea within
our skins as in the sea we swim.
We rhyme with everything that's
   always only what it is
   no matter where it's been or what's
ahead.
         We mime the steady
staying of a boat.
                 We ride
the ballast of our breath.
                       We float.

And Nowhere Shall We Go

Winter's a war we're never
   quite prepared to fight.
It speaks in white surprises,
   drowning us like fear in chorus
   after chorus of itself.
                    Somehow
it makes me dream of everywhere
that leaves life out—corporate
floors partitioned for computers—
military bases—mopped wards
for the incurable.
                   Those Scandinavians
who prance buck-naked
through the snow or swim
in zero lakes fool no one
but themselves.
                We're made for flowers
and no frost—sausages and coffee
in the morning—beaches at noon
with green mountains in the distance.
Last month I watched the leaves
   rise up and plunge full-faced
   toward my knees like children
   fleeing a cyclone.
                Each gust
declared the year an hourglass
that slenders down to shorter days
before it funnels earthward
into April.

        Each leaf announced
    we're all the fading autographs
    of God in different languages . . .
Tonight I'm lying here beside you
    while the wind keeps harvesting
    what straggles in the branches.
                            So
    quietly you sleep, too quietly.
    I fit my palm against
        your ribs and leave it there
        until I feel you breathe.
                      I keep it
there.
        For what?
                For reassurances?
For proof that every breath
    delays whatever end awaits
    the two of us, or, paraphrasing
Donne, the one of us?
                    Who knows . . .
Since love is never free of fearing,
    is it love or just insomnia
    that makes me dream this way?
Or is it only weather
    and the mystery of weather?
                        The snow,
    when it comes, should tell me.

The Vow We Breathe

    Nothing has ever changed
      for me but you and never will.
It's not the years.
              What
    are they but a way (and not
    the best) to count the past?
And what's the past but who
    we've grown to be right now?
And how can that make life
    more sacred or an inch
    less dangerous?
              Our rooms
gaze out on flowers that proclaim
like flags we're here to be
each other's counterpart, and that's
enough.
           And yet to live
together but to die alone
seems so unjust of God
the merciful.
            The mate who's left
goes on but partially, unable
or unwilling to disguise the naked
limp of being incomplete.
The Greeks were wrong.
                Those
whom the gods would destroy
they make at first not mad,
but happy.

                What else
is tragedy, is life?
                If I
could make a toast, I'd say
each breath and not each year's
an anniversary.
                Your rhododendrons
say that every time they bloom.
And so do all your hyacinths,
    azaleas, tulips, dogwoods,
    lilacs and wisterias.
                Because
of you I bless these blossoms
by their names.
                I bless this true
and holy earth that undergirds
us while we live and hides
us when we die.
                I bless
all love that baffles understanding,
human or divine.
                What else
explains how every mate's
a lock one key alone
can open?
            I'm yours.
                You're mine.

Lovemakers

> *Loves mysteries in soules do grow,*
> *but yet the body is his booke.*
>
> John Donne

It's what you feel when you
  become a poem, and you reach
  to sing yourself to her
  whose presence has created you.
Your very lips are words.
                Your hands
  speak sentences.
           Your body
  learns a language it is just
  inventing, touch by touch . . .
She turns from being merely
  naked to the Modigliani nude
  that every woman changes to,
  aroused.
        Her breasts forget
  their future.
            She thinks so
softly with her thighs that not
  a ripple stirs the surfaces
  she swims . . .
              Like figure-skating
  or the last duet from *La Boheme*
  or two in tandem on a bike,
  this double solo will decline
  from ecstasy to prose with one
  mistake.
         Its moments match
  the slow infinity of clouds.
It shows how one plus one

make one in the first,
the best, the ultimate of dances.
Later—but much too soon—when
bodies slacken back to fact,
the sea becomes its sheeted
self again, and all the unrepentant
and abolished clocks reclaim
a time that for a moment scorned them.

One Flesh

All those who wrote of loving,
   even Shakespeare, missed the point.
Describing lips, hair, eyebrows,
   breasts and thighs is not
   enough.
         All this is merely
what's observable, and love
outraces the observable as sight
outraces sound across the universe.
When observation stops and lovers
   act, they are what words
   attempt to say and, saying,
   fail to say.
         The alphabet
of lovers speaks in pauses,
touches, cries and tears
involuntary as a blink and just
as uncontrollable.
         It sails
them through the night
as dreams might sail them
through wing-feather sleep.
It's more than being free
   of underwear and watches, more
   than the stiffening and sheathing
   flesh that lets them bind and bond
   and be what Plato claimed we were
   in the beginning, more even than
   the ecstasies of luck or God

or ecstasy itself.
    It leaves them
animal enough just long
enough to learn the language
of the tiger and the lamb.
     But while
they're one another, they become
a land that no one's mapped
though most have tried—a song
that must be sung to be
the song it is—a time
so free of time that nothing
matters but donating to each other
everything they are . . .
     Spent,
they disengage and lie together
in the loll of after-love
and listen.
    The walls, the air,
the bed become so quietly
important.
    White curtains
ripple like the hushed flags
of peace.
    An over-flying jet
pursues its decrescendo over lights
and silences as reassuring as the stars.

Partings

    Most do it badly; few,
      well.
          All view it as a death
      of sorts—an end at worst,
      at best a change.
                 Grandfathers
    who've outlived their kin
    sit rocking on an empty porch
    and staring, staring . . .
                     Soldiers
    locating military graves
    where men they knew are buried
    suddenly turn old and kneel
    and sob.
          Lovers in separation
    miss, of course, becoming bare
    at loin and nipple in the night
    when fear and doubt a single
    kiss can stifle.
                The hurt's
    the same.
              Why can't we say
    the very hurt that wounds us
    proves us human after all?
                    Or see
    how newer lives begin
    with deaths or births or mere goodbyes?
Instead, we miss that sense
    of youth that life and touch

can give by simply being what
they are.
        Or hunger backward
for that nakedness of face when love
revealed itself in brow,
in lips, in eyes that did not,
would not, could not lie.
                  Or know
at heart that only what we've lost
can find us . . .
            But lost or found,
we face new partings every time
we breathe.
           Even the words
I'm writing now will never be
themselves until I let them go.
Like borrowings that need not be
  repaid, they've won for me
some wisdom and the mercy
of distraction.
             And so I read them
gratefully for what they've said
and what they could not say.
                  And then
I stop and breathe and let them go.

How Married People Argue

    Because they disagreed on nuclear
    disarmament, because he'd left
    the grass uncut, because she'd spilled
    a milkshake on his golfbag,
    he raced ten miles faster
    than the limit.
               Stiffening,
    she scowled for him to stop it.
His answer was to rev it up
    to twenty.
            She asked him why
a man of his intelligence would
take out his ill-temper on a car?
He shouted in the name of Jesus
    that he never ever lost
    his damn temper.
             She told him
he was shouting—not to shout—
that shouting was a sign of no
intelligence.
            He asked a backseat
witness totally invisible
to anyone but him why women
had to act like this.
             She muttered,
"Men," as if the word were mouthwash
she was spitting in a sink.
              Arriving
at the party, they postponed the lethal

  language they were saving for the kill
and played 'Happily married.'
Since all the guests were gorging
on chilled shrimp, the fake went
unobserved.
  She found a stranger's
jokes so humorous she almost
choked on her martini.
    He demonstrated
for the hostess how she could
improve her backswing.
      All the way
home they played 'Married
and so what.'
    She frowned as if
the car had a disease.
      He steered
like a trainee, heeding all
speed limits to the letter,
whistling "Some Enchanted Evening"
in the wrong key, and laughing
in a language only he could
understand.
    At midnight, back
to back in bed, he touched
the tightness of her thigh.
      She muttered,
"I'm asleep," as if her permanent address
were sleep.

                He rose and roamed
        their darkened house, slammed
        every door he passed and watched
        a prison film with George Raft.
Abed at dawn, he heard
        the tears she meant for him
        to hear.
                He listened and lay still.
Because they both had round-trip
        tickets to the past but only
        one-way tickets to the future,
        he apologized for both of them.
They waited for their lives to happen.
He said the hostess' perfume
        was Eau de Turpentine.
                        She said
        the party was a drag—no humor.
Word by word, they wove themselves
        in touch again.
                Then silence
        drew them close as a conspiracy
        until whatever never was
        the issue turned into the nude
        duet that settled everything
        until the next time.

Two Against the Mountain

Surely you have seen us
  spidering our way from piton
  to piton up sheer rock,
  trusting only in our feet
  and fingers and the rope of life
between us.
         We're certain
  of our goal but not the route.
That's something we discover
  inch by inch by listening
  to what the mountain knows.
With both our lives at stake,
  we make a wedding out of work.
Now and again—a word . . .
Otherwise . . . the slow strain
  of reaching sideward to be sure
  before we step but still unsure
  until the step is taken.
Those moments when the outcome
  is in doubt is why we climb.
Connected, we become what
  those who keep each other's
  life in trust become.
            Who knows
the word for this?
            It's waging
both our lives on faith
by pitting all we are against
what cannot be foretold.

It's falling when we fail
    but knowing that whatever held
    or holds the two of us together
    like a vow will hold, will hold.

Embracing Willa

You remembered her tall as her sons
   with browngold hair curled close
   and cut at a slope to her nape.
Now as you bend to pay
   your last respects, she holds you
   tightly as the past, and cries.
She's shorter by a foot.
                    Her hair's
   gone white and thinner.
                    Both sons
   stand by like surrogates, each one
   resembling something in their father
   she's recalling as she lingers
   in your arms.
                    Loosening, she seems
   to lessen and lighten as if
   to say, "I'm shrinking, Sam.
   I'm shrinking."
                    Without a cue
   her fifty-year-old boys assist
   her to her chair.
                    They tend her
   like a daughter who might trip
   or fall.
          Seated, she's Willa
   the queen again, a sentinel
   at either arm, her glasses
   upped like a tiara in her hair.

En Route

    Starting, you memorize the names
    of streets you leave behind.
You tag and tally passing
    neighborhoods, the titles of tunnels,
    and mileage totals clocking by
    like birthdays.
              Nothing, not even
    the long-since struck and stiffening
    doe you swerve to miss, escapes you.
You live sequestered in the fuel-
    injected, air-conditioned country
    of car.
          Mile by minute
    you learn the language of car,
    the Fahrenheit of car, the straight
    philosophy of car . . .
                Midway
    to where you never know you're going,
    you start to think in hours,
    then mornings, afternoons and nights,
    then simply light and dark.
Tunnels become the shortest line
    between two points.
              Towns
    are mere delays.
                Cities announce
    themselves and vanish in your rear-
    view mirror.

        You're closing in
on what you call your destination.
More definite because it's nearer
   now, it loses most of its attraction.
It turns into a problem you will never
   solve.
        Meanwhile, the road
is where your world and all
reality is happening.
             Because
the darts of sleep are numbing you,
you turn the windshield wipers on
and sing along with Pavarotti.
You keep forgetting what you can't
   remember.
          You're like those people
of an age for whom what's most
important is far back or right now.
Like them you know where you began
and where you are this minute.
But in between those sure
   parentheses, you're vague about
   a time which for a time meant
   everything, then nothing—somewhere
   you were and then were not—
   a history—a dream—a life.

All Mirrors Show the World Reversed

    Not just reversed, but altered—
sometimes for the better, sometimes
not.
    A lakeshore duplicated
in a lake is not the shore
we recognize.
        Upside down,
the greens and yellows lengthen
into sunken clouds.
            The plummeting
mountains shimmer in the shallows,
and the drowned jet passes
like a line of print we're just now
reading to completion, left
to right.
        In photographic terms
this way of seeing never moves
beyond the negative.
            The cheek
we soap and shave is not
the cheek we're shaving.
                Mirrored,
a room confronts us
with its opposite.
           We're faced
with nothing but inaccurate
fidelities.
        Why then rebuke
Chagall for painting donkeys
in the sky?

        Or criticize Rouault
for making Christ a clown?
Or scorn Picasso for his world
   where everything presents itself
   in four perspectives all at once?
What more are facts but endings
   we begin with?
        They wait
to be re-born through us
until they turn into the truth
that hides beneath, beyond,
within.
        If we can re-create
them in a different place and time,
we will and do because we can.
Why not?
        It frees us from the perjury
of colored shadows framed
in glass.
        It proves we're here
to make again what God made
once, but differently.
        If we
succeed, we're gods.
        If we
exaggerate, we prove we're not
prepared for wonder.
        If we
give up, we don't deserve
the Christmas of our own amazement.

The Night Before the Snow

   The maple dreams.
               Sleeved
  in its bark-hide, it dreams
  until the kiss of March
  shall rouse it from its zero
  sleep.
          Its knotted roots
  branch down to match beneath
  the trunk what gushers up to end
  in downward criss-cross sprays
  above.
          Its final leaves
  keep scudding into nooks
  and huddling there like cornered
  wrens.
         Leafless or not,
  it stays erect, intact, correct
  and waits for resurrections
  that it knows will come . . .
The propped impatiens tells
  a different story.
              Because
  its only season is the sun,
  it won't survive the night,
  but it's oblivious.
              Lacking
  the maple's built-in horoscope,
  it blooms toward first frost
  when it will blacken all at once . . .

Part maple, part impatiens, I
   dicker with that shrinking dream
   I call the future.
              Three
   thieves await me there.
The sick thief says, "A lingering
   will save you from your usual
   indulgences."
            The sly thief
   snaps, "A sudden silencing
   confounds anticipation and defense."
The old thief mumbles,
   "Age is a wheel that saddens
   slowly to a stop."
            Because
   each thief is right, I'm frozen
   in mid-argument.
            The maple
   in me counters, "Be prepared.
All thieves exist to be
   outsmarted.
            So—outsmart!"
The doomed impatiens whispers
   from its cross, "A flower's born
   to flower, and I'm flowering.
If I should die tonight, I die
   my fullest, ripest best.
If there's a better fate
   than that, what is it?"

Pipedream

On some stone balcony in Mexico
   or France or on your own front porch,
   you peer through pipesmoke at the moon.
It's all the same.
               Caribbean
   spray anoints the beach.
                        The wind's
   cologned with Mediterranean jasmine.
Pittsburgh's a dream with rain
   in the forecast.
                    Because you've seen
   how marvels can be thought
   to death, you watch and listen
   like a witness sworn to silence.
You hear bad Spanish spoken
   by a German chef, children
   arguing in Provençal, a screaming
   woman being tickled long
   enough to plead, "All right,
   all right, I'll go, now stop it,
   stop!"
          The past won't stay
   behind you.
              It settles in the future
   where it's always been.
                   Who was
   the boy you were if not
   a prophecy that's happening?
What else is Hiroshima but a possible

    tomorrow?
           Which way's the world?
It's decades now since 1963,
    but Kennedy just died.
             You know
the long-since gone much better
than you know your brother
or yourself.
          Seeing invisible
flakelets of snow sifting
straight downward by the millions
at the same speed, you
age without regret because
you understand how ageing differs
from decay.
         You feel adrift
on something like a sea, and you're
unsinkable.
           Whatever seemed
unthinkable or totally absurd
has suddenly come true.
            You face
each minute with the same continuous
expectancy of those who could be
lovers.
      That's life enough
for now.
         That's love enough for you.

The Best Place in America to be on Saturdays

    Long live this cafeteria of coiled
      hoses, ladders that open
      as the letter A, canned
      lacquer by the gallon, dangled
      key-shapes waiting to become
      the key, cedar planking
      destined for sanding, staining,
      standing on X-legs beneath
      a bistro tablecloth.
                  Heady
    with hardware, I just can't pass
    unless I touch the trueness
    of a lock.
             Doorknobs rounded
for the human palm tell me
to turn them.
             I grip the ranked
handles of racked rakes
or stacked spades as sluggers
grasp their bats to know them.
Wherever I look, I hear,
   "Use me—I will serve you
well."
         I ponder and agree.
Nothing will ease the hunger
   of a hoe but humus clotted
   to its blade.
              And nothing seems
more primed for glistening

than lightbulbs sleeping
      in their wasp-hive sleeves.
What makes me haggle like a gossip
   here about a hinge, a fuse,
   the tint and texture of cement?
Or talk as earnestly of bevels
   or the level rightness of a walnut
   shelf as if the stakes were grave
   as birthrights or a point of law?
Is it because, no matter
   how I try, I'm never
   wiser than the truth of tools?
New, they're good.
                  Older,
   they're better.
               New or old,
   they make the most of little
   and the best of least.
                  The power
   of a bolt remembers Archimedes
   and the gates of Troy.
                  I can't
   imagine anything more perfect
   for its purpose than a nail.
I wonder if a hammer can be
   bettered, and it can't.
                  I stop
   before a tray of quiet knives
   and look and wait and look.

The knives respond like knives
  being looked at.
      Their sharpness
  wakens in my skin the maker
  I was born to be.
        My hand
  regains its cunning, and the days
  I've yet to live seem suddenly
  as numbered as my hairs.

The Year of the Horse

My father said, "All horses
   when they run are beautiful."
I think of that each time
   I watch Arabians in silhouette,
   the clobbering drays, the jet
   stallions that policemen rein,
   the stilting foals and colts, the sometimes
   bumping always pumping rumps
   of geldings harnessed to a rig.
They prance through war and history:
   "Without the horse the Mongols
   never could have conquered Europe."
And tragedy: "A horse, a horse,
   my kingdom for a horse!"
And sport: "Five minutes
   of hard polo will exhaust
   the strongest horse on earth."
Unsaddled and afoot, how far
   could Cossack, cowboy, Indian
   and cavalier have gone?
                       What made
   so many generals and emperors
   prefer their portraiture on horseback?
What simulacrum but a horse
   succeeded where Achilles failed?
And where did John put hatred,
   famine, pestilence and war
   but on the backs of horses?

                        And that's
not all.
            Pegasus still says
to gravity that poetry's none
other than a horse with wings.
It's not a question of intelligence.
Horses, like poetry, are not
    intelligent—just perfect
    in a way that baffles conquest,
    drama, polo, plough
    and shoe.
                So poem-perfect
    that a single fracture means
    a long, slow dying in the hills
    or, if man's around, the merciful
    aim an inch below the ear.
But when they run, they make
    the charge of any boar at bay,
    the prowl of all the jungle
    cats, the tracking beagle
    or the antelope in panic seem
    ignoble.
                Just for the sake
of the running, the running, the running
they run . . .
                And not another
animal on two or four
or forty legs can match

that quivering of cords beneath
their pelts, the fury in their manes,
the hooves that thump like rapid
mallets on the earth's mute drum,
the exultation of the canter and the gallop
and the rollick and the frolic and the jump.

Vietnam

It's not the monument, sad
 as it is in its black silence.
Not the films—a decade
 late and safely critical.
Not the books the generals
 and senators keep writing
 to exonerate themselves.
Not the Presidents.
 They said
 what all the polls and teleprompters
 scripted them to say.
 Not
 the war we thought we'd win
 for the right reasons but fought
 for the wrong ones.
 Not
 the country that was once
 a headline that became a nightmare
 that remains a contradiction
 that will never die . . .
 It's three
 men under forty slouched
 in wheelchairs in a classroom
 five elections after LBJ.
Their T-shirts speak a lingo
 that is theirs and history's—
 "White Lightning," "King
 of the Mekong Delta," "Eat
 My Dust."

Parting, they aim
their powered wheels at promises
that used to be their lives.
The generation history pretended
they defended separates
before them like a sea.

Whatever Makes It Happen Makes It Last

   This man's a good translator
     but a public fool.
             These clans
     have such a consanguinity of views
     that all their books seem interchangeable.
That one has let her cause
     corrupt whatever poetry
     was hers, and what was hers
     was not dismissable.
             Those two
     have never grown beyond awards
     they won too soon.
             I could
     go on, but what's the point?
Poets are never poetry.
             Who knows
     what wakens fire in the blood
     of saints and sycophants alike?
Who cares?
             The gift's in the awakening—
     in words that flare and flame
     across the white adventure
     of a page.
             If you are one
     so visited, imagine you are
     speaking to an audience.
                Imagine
     every listener is you
     plus ten times fifty.

                    Hearing you
by choice, they compliment you
just by being there.
                    You share
each other as you'd share
the steady goodness of a book,
the sun in all its indiscriminate
democracy, the presence of the very
air.
     Because your listeners
are guests, as you are theirs,
they keep returning you like mirrors
to yourself.
            You stay in touch
with them as lovers stay
in touch, withdrawing only
when the poem they alone have made
returns them to their separate
but undivided lives.
                    But while
in touch, you hold back
nothing.
        You give beyond
the point where giving says enough.
The worst defect is stinginess.

Not Even Solomon . . .

    Whatever you can buy's not valuable
       enough, regardless of the cost.
    What can't be bought's invaluable.
    Not just the white freedom
       of a rose, sparrows in their soaring
       circuses, that girl from Amsterdam
       so tanly tall in Montfleury,
       harbors at noon with clouds
       above them pillowing like snow
       and absolutely still.
                        I'm talking
    love.
       I'm talking love
    and poetry and everything that's true
    of each and interchangeably of both.
Randomly free, they leave
    us grateful to no giver
    we can name.
                    They prove what cannot
    last can last forever even
    when we say it's lost . . .
Some losers ache like Angus
    or like Leila's madman, pining
    for a time so briefly given
    and so quickly gone.
                   Bereft,
    they raise their anguish into songs
    that give a tongue to wounds
    that never heal.

             In every song
       they imitate those troubadours
       whose poems have outlived
       their lives.
                 Forget how far
       they went in school, their ages
       or their kin.
             Whatever wanted
       to be said and wanted only them
       to say it made them what
       they are.
             It turned them
       into words that we can share
       like bread and turn into ourselves.
    They asked, as I am asking now,
       for some less unforgiving way
       to say it, and there isn't.
    Or if what happened once
       might be repeated, and it can't.
    Or if another poet's words
       would say it better, and they don't.
    Or if this cup could pass
       and spare them poetry and all
       its contradictions, and it won't.

The Wait When the Patient Is You

    The cold, flat ear of steel
      above your nipple chills you
      like a touch of ice.
                Slowly
      your body warms it with itself.
    The doctor broods and listens
      to your muffled drum of blood, lung-
      language and the breaths you count
      because they seem more precious now.
    Bad news is what he leans
      to hear.
             How bad?
                   Enough
      to change your life.
                 How good?
    Never as good as he would like.
    His nurse thumps up your vein
      until it's proud enough
      for her to needle out the warm
      maroon into a tube and tray it.
    Wrapping your bicep with a cuff
      of cloth, she pumps it tight
      and reads your mileage on a gauge.
    Now come the X-ray's glow
      and buzz.
                Already you're becoming
    parts you're not the sum of,
    and there's more ahead.
                   You aim
    your kidney's surplus at a fishmouth

    jar and miss and miss and hit.
You watch your knee nod yes
    to hammertaps.
            With every
    test you're more like everybody,
    less like you.
           Who is this man
    you're paying to pronounce you
    fit or fat, explore
    your nethers fore and aft
    and lecture you about triglycerides?
You want the armor of your clothes
    again.
        You want to be entire
    as you were and say out loud
    forthrightly in precise American
    that, after all, you have a name
    and family and work to do and rights.
You feel your seething seethe
    to where he's studying your charts . . .
Oblivious, he tells you the results
    are good.
          You smile.
                You're *you*
  again . . .
        You thank him for his time.
You thank him for your clothes.
He nods and crosses to a sink
    and scrubs his fingernails and goes.

If I Were a Chef, I'd Say

    Buy fresh, cook fresh, eat fresh.
    What's brighter than new mint?
    Better than bread when it's born?
    Younger than breakfast?
                      For me
      it's all one poem, even
      the scraps.
             If you observe me
    in my kitchen dicing onions,
    furling lettuce on a plate,
    or boning yellow sole, you see me
    at my most relaxed.
                   The honesty
    of food does that.
                It's like
    returning to your body after
    you've been thinking much too much
    or like the love you make
    when it's spontaneous and mutual.
You live within your skin and like
    the feeling.
               That's what I'm seeking
    when the world perplexes me
    enough to make me want
    to cook.
             Sidewalk religions
    like jogging perplex me.
                   Fake
    fruits on real tables
    perplex me.

        People who believe
    before they think perplex me . . .
I'd rather speak in coriander,
    garlic, basil, pepper,
    fennel and the herbs of Provençe . . .
With food you can't be fooled.
You cook it with respect to let
    the savors bloom.
           And while
you cook, you think of the convergences.
How many years of breeding
    to create the pork from this pig?
How many months to make
    these peppers, carrots, onions
    and potatoes?
           How much is owed
    to soil, climate, rainfall,
    farmers, butchers, truckers,
    hucksters and the luck of weather?
And what about my forbear's
    forbear's forbear's art passed down
    by blood and hand to mock
    the centuries and make me what
    I am?
        All these present me
    with this roast I'm now arranging
    on a platter like a still-life
    to be eaten with the eyes.
                I ring

   the roast with pepper slivers,
   carrot checkers, onions, skinned
   potatoes and a rosary of parsley.
And there it steams and shines
   for me—the Michelangelo of meat.

The University of All Smiles

    The sleek and Anglo-Saxon Christ
        on all the calendars looks
        vaguely like an ad for beards.
    WGOD is loud with Armageddon,
        cattle prices and the songs
        of Brother Benjamin.
                Splayed
        on my guestroom desk, a Bible,
        bound in lavender leather,
        crinkles with onionskin psalms.
    In the face of so much virtue,
        what can I do but watch
        my step?
                Everyone says
        hello, even the joggers.
    Everyone smiles, even
        the frowners.
                Everyone shows
        what it's like to be saved, even
        the jokers . . .
                Gardens without
        a snake bring out the Holmes
        in me.
            I sniff for a little
        conspicuous vice, but here
        it's hidden like pornography in Mecca.
    Call me obtuse, but I'm on guard
        when good and bad don't co-exist
        as I distrust elections where

    there's no dissent.
                    I'm more
    at peace with Dante's sinner-saints
    than all the kindergartens of Angelico.
So, Brother Benjamin, sing on.
The world may end at three
    o'clock tomorrow afternoon,
    and all who smoke cigars
    may be the devil's spawn.
My world begins and ends
    each time I breathe.
                    I smoke
cigars.
        I sing a different song.

Stingers

    Sluggish and tame, October's
      bees inspect the space
      between my elbow and my pipe.
I welcome the distraction . . .
                      So much
      around me's changed.
                 My first
      time here the Tigers won
      the flag and spared Detroit
      from being torched a second
      time.
         Today the city's
      down a million, sliding
      westward, and the skyline
      flattens into crabgrass-lots
      that once were neighborhoods.
When anyone suggests Detroit
      is prototypical, the mayor
      swears on television . . .
                      Still
      they count the yearly murders
      here the way the Goodyear
      meter totals day by day
      an endless birth of tires.
Earlier I asked a friend,
      "What's your response to urban
      violence?"
              "I keep my pistol
      loaded."

   This from a doctor
of status, taste and means
but with a mind too fortified
to think.
   Why didn't I say
that weapons are the spawn of fear,
that fortress-minds—like all
the forts in history—are destined
for defeat, that waiting for the worst
allows the worst to happen?
My questions circle me like bees
 that may at any moment strike.
The real bees dip and dawdle
 in the sun.
    They seem bemused.
They let me live in their environment,
 not mine.
    In time they'll do
what bees must do and sting.
The poison's there and waiting.

Six-Sevenths

July times sixty equals nothing
  but July.
        Still me, still one
of billions on the spun spins
we number as we go, I'm just
the progeny of accidents parenthesized
by accident.
        The Bible of the Jews
proclaims the final seventh
of my span's upon me.
           Walking
where the dead outlive us,
and the sky and sea persist
eternally as God, and history's
a billow from a fool's cigar,
I seem the same.
        What locks me
in the totally exact distracts me
with the facts, but what's the point?
Today I watched a crippled
  docent talking Marc Chagall
alive for twenty girls and seven
boys.
      Her words were wands.
Her wheelchair flew her as she spoke,
  and all the children's faces
blossomed into stars.
         The time
of paint became the only
time she saw.

          She said
the drawings of Chagall were dreams
where horses dance, and Christ
has yet to die, and Isaac
slumbers like his mother's laughter
on the altar of the Lord.
                    She might
as well have said we live
no truer than our hopes, and that
our dreams can bloom as scarlet,
indigo and yellow scriptures
that will save the world.
                        Which
world?
      The one we wake to
or the one we make?
                    Or both?
Or neither?
            God of our final
hopes, is contradiction after
contradiction all that we create
before our lives abandon us?
The years behind me keep accumulating
    like a surf that's mounting, mounting
    for its final, disappearing surge.
What can I do but carry on
    like everybody, questioning myself
    until I drown in reason, dreaming
    like Chagall, and counting, counting?

Putting Away the Lost Summer

The swing's unslung and winter-waxed,
 the mint leaves waiting to be sieved
 to salt, the hose unscrewed
 and coiled like a rattler in the shed.
As usual the ripening figs
 will blacken at first frost
 exactly as they did last year
 when all the talk was war.
This year the human harvest
 makes the war seem dim:
 one suicide, three deaths, one
 shock, one disappointment and a swindle.
Each one bequeathed its epitaph:
 "Your letter was a narrow bridge
 to the rest of my life."
         "He didn't
 recognize me, Sam—his own
 sister."
      "I'll stay until he's well
 or else not here any more."
Remembering, I see how much
 can never be the way it was,
 despite appearances.
             Philosophy's
 no help.
      Religion's even less.
And poetry does nothing but re-live
 what's lost without redeeming it
 like life's exact revenge

    upon itself.
           What's left
    but learning to survive with wounds?
Or studying the fate of figs
    before the unexpected chill,
    not knowing in advance how many
    or how few will be destroyed
    or toughened when it comes . . .
Playing for time, I occupy
    myself with chores and tools,
    uncertain if the lot I've chosen
    is a gambler's or a coward's or a fool's.

Your Death Is in the Making as You Make Your Life

September's sculpting you.
                       Each
week's a chisel or a flint,
each day a casting free
of chaff, each night a reason
to be rid of dross.
                   Reasons
ago, September sculpted
Saundra into silence—Saundra
who sang in Monaco with Calloway
and laughed a laugh that filled
a room like victory.
                    Sudden
as cardiacs or slower than the pangs
of loss, September pares away
and pares away.
                Even these words
are paring you from who you were
to who you are.
                 There's no
relief . . .
             If death's within,
and life's abreast of you
or just ahead, you live and die
in opposite directions.
                   Growing,
you diminish.
              Diminishing,
you grow into yourself as quietly

as burls of maples wizen
into stone.
         On balance, it's
ridiculous.
         Each day you struggle
to achieve impossible perfections
while every day you're being
sculpted back to bone.
         And all
the time you're at the mercy
of a sudden, interrupting insult
aimed for centuries at you alone . . .

The Most You Least Expect

You think of photographic paper
drowning in developer.
                Slowly
the whiteness darkens into forms.
Shadows become a face;
the face, a memory; the memory,
a name.
        The final clarity
evolves without a rush
until it's there.
            It's like
your struggle to remember
what you know you know
but just can't quite recall.
No matter how you frown,
the secret stays beyond you.
You reach.
        It moves.
                You reach
again.
        Again it moves.
It's disobedience itself, but still
it wants so much to be regained
by you, only by you.
                Later,
when it lets itself be known,
you wonder how you ever could
have lost so obvious a thing.
And yet you take no credit

    for retrieving it.
                It came to you
on its own terms, at its
own time.
        You woke, and it
was there like love or luck
or life itself and asked
no more of you than knowing
it by name.
            The name is yours
to keep.
        You burn to share
this sudden and surprising gold
with everyone.
            You feel the glee
of being unexpectedly complete
and sure and satisfied and chosen.

At Midnight There Are No Horizons

1

    The suckle-skin that slakes
    the smallest thirst is fed
    by what is sucking it.
            Tightly
    bonded at the loins, all lovers
    flex and thrust in ditto
    ravenings they rouse
    and satisfy and, satisfying, rouse
    again.
        Pre-skeletal, we're
    at the mercy of our mouths.
Or are we merely one
    another's food as God is ours?
Beneath the world of the polite,
    the meekly conscientious or the quietly
    predictable, we vie with deeper
    hungers.
          Hungering, we're like a bride
    who shucks her slip and under-
    silks and lets herself be loved
    into a new geography.
            Her final
    whimpers wake her like a field
    that lightning suddenly ignites
    into the height and depth and breadth
    of what it means to *be*.

                    Or
we can rise like Cain and kill
a brother who will be no less
a brother in his grave.
                    What good's
philosophy if what we are
is what we are?
              How holy
are religions if we've killed for God
as readily as for revenge
or jealousy or just the hell of it?
On days as brief as pleasure
   or as long as sorrow, we concede
as feeder or as food that all civility's
a lie, and everything from love
to murder is a twitch of appetite.

2

    Death hides in every clock,
      and so we damn them all.
    They keep reverting us to bone
      or else to relics that re-live us . . .
    Dour drunk deadman's gone
      to the angels.
               Gone too
    the southern cavalier who sang
    of war and bats and what
    it meant to wither.
              Gone
    last the lanky king
    who lorded wide his royalty
    by cunning, craft and kin
    until he paced the stage alone.
What are they now but pages
    on a small, tight shelf of books?
Each one keeps to his inches.

3

    Clockmakers from Ticino say
      that every minute wounds us,
      and the last one kills.
                 Wounded
      every day but still undead,
      we breathe behind last words—
      "All else being equal . . ." or "Nine
      chances out of ten . . ." or "Barring
      the unforeseeable."
                   We learn
      too late that nothing's equal
      here, that single chances are the most
      we get, that everything is unforeseeable.
    The poem of our lives proclaims
      there's something still ahead
      to be discovered if we just have time.
    Rush, and we miss it.
                   Wait,
      and it finds us.
               Even
      while we notch initials in a birch,
      have schools or sons or streets
      named after us, endow cathedrals
      to remember us in bronze, the poem
      of our lives is always being
      born.

We are the picture
it's creating, breath by breath.
What's taking shape is never
what we planned and not what we expect.
We call it life because we must.
We have it just where it wants us.